THE ROSE GARDEN

Climbing Roses

ELVIN McDONALD

THE ROSE GARDEN

Climbing Roses

SMITHMARK

ELVIN McDONALD

This edition published by Smithmark Publishers,
a division of U.S. Media Holdings, Inc., 115 West
18th Street, New York, NY 10011.

Smithmark books are available for bulk purchase
for sales promotion and premium use. For
details, write or call the manager of special sales,
Smithmark Publishers, 115 West 18th Street, New
York, NY 10011.

TEXT & PHOTOGRAPHY: Elvin McDonald
DESIGN: Stephen Fay
SERIES EDITOR: Kristen Schilo, Gato & Maui
Productions

Printed and bound in Hong Kong

10 9 8 7 6 5 4 3 2 1

ISBN: 0-7651-9063-X

McDonald, Elvin.
        Climbing roses / Elvin McDonald.
            p. cm. — (Rose garden series)
        ISBN 0-7651-9063-X (alk. paper)
        1. Climbing roses.   I. Title.   II. Series:
            McDonald, Elvin. Rose garden series.
        SB411.65.C55M34   1999
        635.9´33734—dc21   98-36130
                                        CIP

DEDICATION

For
Janis

*Thanks especially
to Carol Hendrick of Brenham, Texas,
for helping edit the pictures at the outset,
to Hilary Winkler of San Francisco,
my research assistant,
who helped sort the words at the end,
to Dave Kvitne,
who actually dug the beds
and planted the roses in my garden…
and
to the gardeners
who permitted me to photograph
in their gardens…*

✺

Climbing Roses and its three sibling books from *The Rose Garden* series, *Tea Roses, Shrub Roses,* and *Old-Fashioned Roses,* have their beginnings in the first rose I planted at age five, about fifty-five years ago, but most specifically in the season (1985) when it was my privilege to work for days and weeks alongside world-class rosarian Stephen Scanniello in the Cranford Rose Garden at the Brooklyn Botanic Garden. Later, I grew and sold roses in Houston, Texas, and I am now in the process of planting my own rose garden in West Des Moines, Iowa. Book teammates, publisher Marta Hallett, series editor Kristen Schilo, and designer Stephen Fay, helped make my *Color Garden* series, *Red, White, Blue,* and *Yellow,* an international success. *The Rose Garden* series is written in the same spirit, to say the big things about a complex subject in a small book.

Contents

Romance

CLIMBING ROSES ARE TO THE ENHANCEMENT of a garden as wallpapers and fabrics are to the decoration of a room. In the vast world of plants, there is nothing quite like the effect of a climbing rose. Not only can it cover or embellish garden structures, it can turn the most ordinary wood arbor or pipe framework into a real-life, fragrant bower of roses that carries the eyes and spirit upward.

Indoors, the decorator uses glue, nails, screws, and stitches to assist in holding things together. Outdoors, climbing roses also need assistance, at least until they become established. As compared to the way some other plants climb, roses are more thrusters and leapers into the air. The gardener sees in this behavior the opportunity to guide and shape the destiny of every promising cane. For example, tying canes to a support can also result in more blooms. Getting the most out of a climbing rose requires a certain amount of patience and the vision to see what might be achieved by tying one cane this way, another that, in order to maximize the potential.

AT LEFT: 'Sombreuil' (1850), a climbing tea, is fragrant, with a white and yellow bloom.
AT RIGHT: *Rosa mulliganii* bowers the White Garden at Sissinghurst in the early summer.

8

Romance

CLOCKWISE FROM LEFT: Old-fashioned rambler roses are trained in a tunnel at Planting Fields, Oyster Bay, New York— 'Crimson Rambler' predominates. In the Harriet Glass Pavilion in the Cranford Rose Garden, Brooklyn Botanic Garden, a large-flowered climbing rose in silvery pink captures the late afternoon light. It shows how even one cane can have a beautiful effect on the architecture of the garden. 'Coral Dawn,' from American breeder Gene Boerner, 1952, has large, high-centered, fragrant blooms. Cold-hardy and everblooming, not to mention sturdy, dark green foliage, 'Coral Dawn' is a superb modern climbing rose. 'Golden Showers,' from American breeder Walter Lammerts, 1956, is one of the most loved large-flowered yellow climbers and, along with 'Zephirine Drouhin,' one of those rare roses that will grow on a north wall.

BELOW: 'Kiftsgate,' a sport from *Rosa filipes,* known in cultivation since 1938, can grow to 40 feet in record time. Individual corymbs can contain hundreds of small, white, fragrant blooms. 'Kiftsgate' is a great rose for climbing into a large tree. AT RIGHT: 'Constance Spry' is a spring-blooming English rose that can grow to 20 feet and is ideal for training on a tripod. OPPOSITE: 'Yellow Lady Banks' varies from cream to an intense yellow, depending on the climate and the temperature at bloom time.

In addition to thrusting and leaping into the air, climbing roses use their thorns like a mountain climber's toeholds. There are also climbing roses that are thornless or nearly so, which makes them ideal for wrapping porch rails and posts.

One of the strongest climbing roses is the sport of *Rosa filipes* known as 'Kiftsgate.' The original plant, obtained by Mrs. Muir of Kiftsgate Court in 1938, is now beyond 60 feet wide and 40 feet tall. However crushing that may sound, 'Kiftsgate' is adorned with a staggering number of fragrant flowers and is still recommended for planting in the company of a large tree.

Vying with 'Kiftsgate' is the rose from West China found on the arbor in the White Garden at Sissinghurst. Known until recently in the nursery trade as *Rosa longicuspis*, it was recently named *R. mulliganii*. The creamy white flowers, in corymbs of up to 150, are abundantly fragrant and become small, orange-red hips in the fall.

An even more fabled climbing rose from China is the 'Yellow Lady Banks,' *Rosa banksiae lutea*, often grown purposely on an oak or hackberry tree. It was first flowered in England in 1824 and has long been a staple in gardens having mild winters (Zones 8-10). If this rose grows in your area, watch to see how big it gets, then site accordingly.

David Austin's English roses are a much more recent arrival. They are numerous, exuberant growers if not outright climbers, and their old-fashioned appearance and availability have won many friends.

A surprising attribute of the Austin roses, despite their origins in the relatively benign climate of England, is that they do well in most American gardens. Granted, in Zones 5 and colder they are more likely to survive winters if grown on their own roots rather than grafted. Their reputation for achieving greater heights in America than in England is well founded, especially where summer means high temperatures both day and night. Happily, this can turn a bush into a climber.

There are two types of climbing rose—the climber and the rambler—with countless variations and exceptions. Climbers, often, but not always have large flowers on stiffer stems and repeat bloom. Ramblers have small flowers in clusters on smaller, more lax stems, and bloom once yearly, but there are exceptions to these rules.

While climbers may be old roses, English roses, sports of modern hybrid teas, or bred as modern climbers, there will always be something about any one of them—large size or form—that distinguishes it from a rambler. Ramblers do have smaller flowers, but in corymbs of an unbelievable number of blooms, and they often have in their parentage the species *Rosa wichuraiana* or *R. multiflora*. Those having white or pink, single flowers recall those of another member of the rose family, the apple. The observant eye may also see in them the blossoms of other family members such as the pear, raspberry, and even the strawberry, usually white, sometimes rose-pink.

ABOVE LEFT: 'Etain' is a 19th century rambler. The large, lightly scented flowers have many rounded petals. AT LEFT: 'Leontine Gervais' is a wichuraiana rambler with the fragrance of its other parent, a tea rose. RIGHT: 'Zephirine Drouhin,' a climbing Bourbon, has fragrance, a long season, and thornless shoots.

RIGHT: 'Excelsa' ramblers and other climbing roses grow on double arches across the main walkways at the Cranford Rose Garden, Brooklyn Botanic Garden, in Brooklyn, New York. They become the quintessential bowers of roses in late spring and early summer.

Verticality

ONE OF THE QUICKEST WAYS TO FEEL you have a garden is to build an arch or arbor and plant climbing roses. This declaration of verticality may seem daring at first, but it will reassure you over and over again with the visual pleasure it offers.

At River Farm on the Potomac, the American Horticultural Society's headquarters in Alexandria, Virginia, 'American Pillar' roses grow up red brick pillars, then reach high above the walkway to the other side on rough-hewn timbers. For part of the year, it is the structures and the thorny canes that make the garden a hopeful place, but when the roses bloom in June, the garden is transformed into a magical place.

Double archways are repeated along the main walks through the Cranford Rose Garden. Planted with a variety of different climbing roses in complimentary colors, the gardens are beautiful to see, to smell, and to walk through. The rosarians have wisely gotten diversity on the double arches by planting different roses that flatter each other. They might also have planted compatible vines such as clematis and honeysuckle, but then it would have been a flower garden, not a rose garden. The different colors, sizes, and mingling scents make it a heavenly place.

RIGHT: The Bourbon rose 'Zephirine Drouhin' has been grown since 1868 and is known for outstanding performance and for flowering continuity. It remains one of the most loved climbing roses.

Ever since King Louis XIV built the elaborate lattice structures at Versailles, more than 200 years ago, gardeners have been inspired to build smaller versions, expressly to show off climbing roses. The openness of lattice walls, arbors, pergolas, and pavilions allows for plenty of light and also assures that the roses growing on them will enjoy good air movement which reduces the likelihood of disease and spider-mite infestations.

Because of the strength of climbing rose canes, lattice needs to be as strong as possible. Prefabricated panels, available in both wood and plastic, will stand up best and be aesthetically acceptable if they are soundly framed and attached to firmly anchored posts. Panels can be customized by cutting out and framing round, oval, or rectangular "windows." It's a better policy to tie the canes in place; lacing them in and out of lattice openings is temptingly expeditious but all too often the roses' expanding growth can rip apart the lattice.

Plastic lattice is a recent innovation that makes the most elegant of garden structures both affordable and long-lasting. Panels in square and diagonal patterns are available at home improvement centers. They come with classic openings as well as smaller ones for more privacy and in a variety of plant-friendly colors that never have to be painted.

AT LEFT: 'Blaze' is a repeat-flowering wichuraiana hybrid that looks stunning on white lattice.
ABOVE: 'Climbing Queen Elizabeth' is a cold-hardy grandiflora with a reputation for vigor and nonstop production of big, beautiful, silvery pink roses.
AT RIGHT: Creamy, fragrant, spring-blooming 'City of York' (left in photograph) and the fragrant, everblooming 'New Dawn' trained on double arches over a path are the personification of romance at their peak and bloom in early summer.

Prefabricated lattice comes in unfinished wood or, if plastic, in white, dark green, or several other colors. Though lattice and treillage have their beginnings in formal French garden design, if it is a more casual setting you want to achieve, then leaving the wood to age naturally will more likely suit. Painting or staining can add color that makes the garden attractive in all seasons and can bring out the glory of the roses themselves. If white or dark green are too extreme, garden designers will typically choose a muted French blue or sagey green for the arbor, both of which are flattering to flowers.

If a climbing rose is to grow on a lattice panel in front of a wall, install it about six inches out from the surface to assure adequate air movement. If the wall requires access for maintenance in the future, to be painted for example, use hinges at the bottom and attach the top with hooks and eyes. When necessary, the lattice panel can be unhooked and leaned back sufficiently to make the wall accessible without harming the rose canes.

A time-honored and delightful way to enjoy climbing roses is to attach them directly to a wall. This works best where little or no maintenance will be required, usually on brick or stone. Install bolts or masonry nails that extend out at least a couple of inches from the wall; tie the canes to these, leaving just enough slack for growth and slight movement.

Climbing roses trained into a vertical plane have height and width but relatively little depth. This is also the idea behind traditional espalier training of a variety of woody plants, in particular fruit trees such as apple and pear. A difference is that roses are less suited to formalized patterns such as palmette verrier and Belgian fence; instead, they are at their best framing windows and doors or fanning out in a more casual way as wall covering. There is also the reality that after several years the oldest, flowered canes will need to be removed at the base and extricated from the younger ones so as to boost strong new basal shoots.

AT LEFT: 'Blaze,'
introduced in 1932, was the
first hardy red-flowered,
everblooming climber.

ABOVE: 'Maigold' has golden yellow flowers
blushed orange. One of the Scotch shrub
roses, it is a thrifty climber with sturdy stems
replete with reddish-brown thorns.

24   *Verticality*

Wrapping a pillar or post with a climbing rose is a delightful way to express verticality. Sometimes a dead tree can be transformed by this means: Cut it back to six or eight feet and leave branch stubs to help support the canes. As the canes grow, wrap them around as a means of horizontalization. If canes are left free at the top, a weeping tree-form can develop. Each year, remove any dead growth and the oldest, flowered canes. A row of pillars set 12 feet apart can be connected with ropes; select long canes at the top to wrap the ropes and form festoons that swoop from pillar to pillar.

LEFT: At Manor House Upton Grey in England, a garden designed by Gertrude Jekyll has been restored and the specially trained climbing and rambling roses set out for lavish display in the meadow.
RIGHT, ABOVE: Double wire trellis arches create a magical architectural effect. BELOW: Modern climbing roses 'America' (salmon-pink) and 'Royal Gold,' both fragrant, adorn a classic arch.

If you must garden in small spaces, climbing miniatures can fill the bill superbly. It's true, some of them can in time grow quite large. However, they can be managed nicely in cramped quarters and even grown in large pots on a city terrace or patio where regular climbers would be completely out of scale. Since they are smaller in all parts, climbing miniatures adapt well to less massive trellises and walls.

Tripods, quadripods, tepees, and tuteurs are currently in vogue as a means of giving the garden verticality. With or without climbing roses, they add interest. The basic configuration for a pyramidal effect from climbing roses is to set two or three feet apart from each other three pipes or wood posts that are eight to twelve feet long. Drive each into the ground about a foot, then pull together and tie at the top. Plant all the same or three different kinds of bushes and tie the canes in a gentle upward spiral, which will induce the maximum number of lateral flowering branches.

Dead wood can be removed at any time from all climbers. Otherwise, roses that bloom once yearly need to have the oldest, flowered canes removed, following the current season's bloom. New canes will then need to be directed and tied in place as often as necessary.

Sometimes as a gardener or property owner one is faced with the daunting task of rehabilitating an old climbing rose that has become a massive entanglement of canes. Arm yourself with impenetrable gauntlet gloves, pruners, and loppers. Work slowly, be deliberate—and persist.

AT LEFT: 'Dortmund,' from Kordes of Germany, 1955, is lightly scented and repeat flowering. Hardy and suited to every type of training, it makes an arresting pillar.

BEGINNING CLIMBERS

CLIMBING ROSES *can be planted any time the soil can be worked and the plants are available. If bare root, they will be shipped at the proper planting time in early spring. Potted specimens, available from local nurseries, let you see which blooms you like best and also give a preview of leaf and cane color.*

Climbers need deeply spaded, well-drained soil, and a site with at least a half day's direct sun. Water in generously and thereafter if dry.

ABOVE: Twig fences and structures are a natural for supporting climbing roses. There is a visual bonus when contrasting the delicate rose with rustic wood. AT RIGHT: 'American Pillar' easily wraps and festoons a standard split-rail fence.

Pairings

LIKE STRAWBERRIES AND SHORTCAKE or gin and tonic, climbing roses always go better when paired. The partner can be architecture, a tree, another rose, or a different, but compatible, plant.

In the wild, it is not unusual to see a rose such as the Cherokee topped out over a tree several stories high. Usually it is the smaller, cluster-flowered climbers that work best with a tree, for example: 'Alberic Barbieri' (creamy white, for mild climates), 'Bloomfield Courage' (single red, early-blooming rambler, a wichuraiana hybrid), 'Chevy Chase' (red rambler), 'Climbing Cecile Brunner' (pale pink sport of a polyantha). 'Seagull' (white, fragrant, multiflora hybrid rambler), and 'Veilchenblau' (violet-blue multiflora rambler).

Also recommended are the larger flowered 'Complicata' (single pink), 'Christine Wright' (pink), 'Mermaid,' and 'Silver Moon.' Perhaps prettiest of all is combining two climbers of the same or similar color, one single, one double, one quite small, the other big.

AT LEFT: 'Mermaid,' though it honors a sea nymph, leaps 20 and 30 feet skyward into the limbs of trees.
AT RIGHT: 'Yellow Lady Banks' appears delicate as a single flower spray up close, but the plant can literally commandeer a tree, dead or alive.

28

Pairings

To grow a climbing rose on a tree, set the plant at the drip line, then install a long bamboo cane. Tilt the cane to a likely branch and train the climber along its length until lift-off is achieved. Eventually, the cane will not be needed and can be removed and discarded.

Don't worry about pruning airborne roses, except possibly to extricate a dead branch. Occasionally, a climbing rose is planted next to the trunk of a tree that has high limbs, with the lowermost branches at a height of 15-20 feet, southern pine is a good example with the canes wound around its trunk in an ever upward spiral.

One way to make the best of a dying or dead tree is to let a climbing rose cover it, that is if the wood of the tree is firm and there is no internal rot that could cause it to come crashing down. Presumably this will also be a small- to medium-sized tree that can be thinned out and pruned back so it will only take the rose a couple of years to give complete and luscious coverage.

ABOVE: Large-flowered clematis, such as 'Dr. Ruppel,' come in every color nuance imaginable, except orange, and can look all the more glorious twining upward with almost any rose. OPPOSITE: Vertical purple-blue spires of delphinium and the herbaceous *Clematis* x *durandii* are potential best bedmates for climbing roses.

One great talent of climbing roses is that they can provide color in a vertical plane that matches, contrasts, or harmonizes with bush roses or other flowers in a more horizontal plane. They can be trained against a wall or lattice fencing, as backdrop to other plantings, or brought out into the open on pillars, in festoons, or wound about a tepee or tuteur as a vertical accent.

Possibly the single best all-around companion for climbing roses is the clematis. Imagine, for example, the pale pink and bounteous climbing 'New Dawn' laced through on a high wall with 'Perle d'Azur' clematis. In practical terms, some of the most beautiful roses that bloom once in late spring and early summer need something to make them more attractive later on; such roses include 'Albertine,' 'Maigold,' and 'Meg.' Perfect companions for these are the large hybrid clematis, as well as the alpina and viticella varieties.

Clematis x *durandii*, because it is herbaceous and cut back near the ground each spring, makes a perfect accent in front of a climbing rose when trained on a small, twig tuteur, which may also be called a tepee or obelisk. If this stands about four or five feet high and is a foot or so in diameter at ground level, the clematis will make an elegant show by late spring.

TAKE TWO ROSES...

ONE OF THE MOST *rewarding ways to enjoy climbing roses is to plant two together whose color or form add to each other's beauty. The large-flowered 'Christine Wright' with its big double pink flowers looks all the more splendid in the company of the single, appleblossom-pink rambler 'Evangeline.'*

One of the most romantic duets between roses is the creamy 'White Cap,' an everblooming pillar, with 'Parade,' which has large, dark pink Bourbon-like flowers. 'White Cockade' and 'Seagull' are nice for a summer shower of pure white. Another winning duo is the rambler 'May Queen' and the large-flowered climber 'Caroline Testout.'

ABOVE: 'Ballerina,' a hybrid musk, looks superb with any red rose. AT RIGHT: 'White Cap,' from Brownell, 1954, and the more recent 'J.C. Connell,' are among the hardiest of all large, white climbers.

The newly popular 'Compassion' climbing rose, which produces heavenly pink to apricot flowers, is superb with a similarly strong-growing clematis such as 'Lawsoniana,' or the shorter 'Hagley Hybrid' or 'Comtesse de Bouchaud.' 'Compassion,' introduced in 1974, is recurrent-blooming and fragrant, and is excellent for cutting.

An irresistible combo is a 'Golden Showers' rose with any blue clematis, such as 'Perle d'Azur,' 'General Sikorski,' or 'Lasurstern.'

'Pink Perpetué' climbing rose with its phosphorescent carmine-pink coloring looks marvelous with the purple clematis 'Jackmanii.'

'Mermaid' may be slow to get going, but eventually when it is high above the garden, nothing could bring out its big, yellow, single flowers better than 'Perle d'Azur' clematis.

Some clematis are too vigorous even for strong climbing roses, *C. montana* for example, and the sweet autumn clematis.

If you like your garden to give a sense of abundance and not too formal, don't hesitate to combine roses and honeysuckle, roses and hardy passion vine or, in the South, roses and jasmine.

AT RIGHT: 'Blairii No. 2' was introduced in England prior to 1843, and has long canes for wrapping pillars or elegantly draping a wall as pictured here, setting off foxgloves.

Choices

CHOOSING THE RIGHT CLIMBER can be intimidating if you consider how much attention the flowers will command when at peak in a few years. It's not as though they will be on tidy bushes in prim beds. A vigorous climber almost flies and when tied down can take on such unexpected shapes as that of a house, an arbor, or a boulder.

Besides cold and heat tolerance, climbing roses can be sorted according to whether they bloom once yearly or all season, and have single or double flowers, with or without an appreciable scent. Some have colorful fall foliage and red or orange hips that persist into winter, brightening the scene and delighting birds.

Of all the variables that affect the choice of a climbing rose, none is more critical than that of cold hardiness where winter means periods of subzero temperatures. 'Viking Queen' (University of Minnesota, 1963), a clear, bright, fragrant pink repeats and qualifies. Two others are 'J.C. Connell' (white) and 'Rhode Island Red' (Brownell, 1957).

FAR LEFT: Fragrant at all stages, until the petals fall, 'Zephirine Drouhin,' a nearly thornless, climbing bourbon, from Bizot, 1873, is reliable into Zone-5 cold. LEFT: 'Graham Thomas' can be a superb choice for garden effect or cutting.

37

The multiflora rose is a good example of why it pays to do some research before planting any climbing rose. Believing such claims that "living fences" will do nearly as much for you as winning the lottery can sometimes lead to disappointment.

There are places, however, where *Rosa multiflora* is welcome. Along roadways it is opportunistic enough—with the help of birds who drop its seeds—to be among the first colonizers after an area is disturbed. On a large property with outbuildings and hedgerows, *R. multiflora* may be present without any particular encouragement. While the true wild multiflora has little or no place in formal or town settings, many of its hybrids—the multiflora ramblers—are perfect.

The rambler's advantage are its long, pliable canes, easily coaxed into assuming the shape or form on which they are trained. In a series of archways, they form a tunnel that is refreshingly cooler in summer and wondrous after a winter snowfall.

Where recurrent bloom and fragrance are desired, some of the best climbers include: 'Compassion' (pink/apricot), 'Dreaming Spires' (yellow), 'J.C. Connell' (white), 'Malaga' (rose pink), 'Madame Alfred Carrière' (white), 'Schoolgirl' (apricot), 'Souvenir de Claudius Denoyel' (crimson), and 'New Dawn' (pearl pink).

ABOVE: *Rosa multiflora* at the edge of a parking lot can be grand. Plant it in a small garden however, and you will be sorry. AT LEFT: After new canes are tied in, the tunnel of ramblers at Butchart Gardens near Victoria, British Columbia, offers an enticing passage.

AT RIGHT: At the
Sutter Home
Vineyards rose
garden, in Sutter
Home Winery, St.
Helena, California,
climbing roses
bower a gazebo.
Irrigated in the dry
summers, they
bloom ten out of
twelve months.

AT RIGHT: 'Tausendschon' rambler, trained as a pillar at the Cranford Rose Garden, shows why it is said that every blooming branch constitutes a virtual bouquet of multicolored roses.

ABOVE: The tea-scented 'Blush Noisette,' introduced in 1817, with pink buds that open into nearly white flowers, makes a show against the walls of a dilapidated garden house. AT RIGHT: *Rosa laevigata* 'Silver Moon' is a 1910 hybrid of the fabled Cherokee rose. Large and fragrant, it is magic in the evening garden.

The delightfully French-named Noisette class of roses had its beginnings in the Charleston, South Carolina, gardens of a rice planter named John Champneys. His mating of *Rosa chinensis* 'Old Blush' with *Rosa moschata*, the musk rose, produced a seedling so promising that he shared it in the early 1800s with his neighbor, nurseryman Philippe Noisette. Noisette, in turn sent the bud wood to his brother in Paris. Named 'Champney's Pink Cluster,' there was soon to be another, 'Blush Noisette,' first recorded in 1817.

Before the end of the 19th century, there would be many Noisettes. A few survivors have become legendary among climbing roses: 'Aimée Vibert' (1828; nearly thornless, climbs, double white flowers), 'Bouquet d'Or' (1873; vigorous, to 10 feet, quartered, double, salmon and yellow flowers), 'Rêve d'Or' (1869), 'Madame Alfred Carrière' (1879; to 20 feet, double pink flowers fade white; blooms right through mild winters), and 'Marechal Niel' (1864; to 15 feet, double, yellow, fragrant flowers), an all-time favorite in the South.

'Jaune Desprez' (also called 'Desprez a Fleurs Jaunes'), was introduced in 1835 from a cross of 'Blush Noisette' by 'Park's Yellow China.' It is a vigorous climber with light green foliage and repeats with fruit-scented yellow-orange-buff flowers.

FLOWER POWER

CLIMBING ROSES *can have a surprisingly softening effect on such harsh realities as utilities meters. If large enough to give the air conditioner window unit ample circulation, a rose-covered lattice screen can at least bring visual pleasure, if not obscure the noise.*

Large-flowered hybrids such as 'Climbing Tropicana' can reach the eaves of a house in a single season. The more they can be bent toward a horizontal rather than vertical position, the greater the potential for lots of flowers.

One of the most beautiful white, fragrant, climbing roses is the 1830 Noisette 'Lamarque.' Possessed of few thorns, it also has little tolerance for cold; out of the Deep South, 'Lamarque' must be coddled over winter in a cool greenhouse. In fact, the Noisettes as a class fare best in warmer regions.

'Rêve d'Or,' a Noisette developed by Ducher of France and released in 1869, continues today as an outstanding climbing rose for mild-climate gardens. The color of the flowers, subtly blending buff and yellow with pink tinges, sits most comfortably with the often muted colors of heritage paints and old bricks in hues softened by time.

'Alister Stella Gray' (1894), also known as the Golden Rambler, opens quite yellow and soon fades to cream. Tea-scented, intermittent-flowering, nearly thornless—an irresistible package for a mild-climate garden.

Peter Beales, one of the 20th century's foremost rosarians, says that the Noisettes have proved hardier to cold in his Norfolk, England, garden than they have been credited. Where temperatures stay above zero, try one or two in a protected spot.

ABOVE, FROM LEFT: 'Lamarque,' 1830, needs a warm climate. 'Rêve d'Or,' 1869, is insinuated into the lattice walls and arbors at the Birmingham, Alabama, Botanic Garden.

Selects

COLORS FOUND IN CLIMBING ROSES vary from clear and primary to all the pastels associated with ice cream, sorbet, and sherbet. Contrasting values and colors have a more exciting effect, while harmonizing and paled-down versions are more calming. The glowing orange 'Climbing Tropicana' could have a jarring effect on the innocence of 'New Dawn.' Mingling any creamy white with any red is likely to bring forth sighs.

When it comes to selecting the right color for a climbing rose one hopes will prosper, nothing compares to observing a specimen in bloom on display at a neighborhood nursery. If house or other structural paint colors are to be factored in, bring swatches to compare or, better yet, purchase the plant so you'll be able to carry it around your garden to get a realistic impression.

Among the best recurrent bloomers and their colors are these: 'Altissimo' (bright red), 'Bantry Bay' (pink), 'Golden Showers' (bright yellow), 'J.C. Connell' (white), 'Mermaid' (sulfur yellow), 'Parade' (carmine red), 'Pink Perpetue' (carmine pink), 'New Dawn' (pink), 'Summer Wine' (dark pink), and 'Zephirine Drouhin' (carmine pink).

AT LEFT: 'Yellow Lady Banks' blooms once yearly; huge old substructure canes send off graceful young flowering wands. AT RIGHT: 'Rêve d'Or' (France, 1869), in an elusive buff color, is very fragrant, and it repeats.

44

AT LEFT, AT RIGHT: David Austin's English rose 'Abraham Darby' is hardly containable as a shrub yet it makes a superb climber, seen here from two angles in a private Columbus, Ohio, garden.
BELOW: 'Climbing Peace' is exceptionally cold-hardy (so too are the climbing forms of 'Iceberg,' 'Queen Elizabeth,' and 'Yesterday').

AT RIGHT:
'Climbing Don
Juan' is noted for its
form and fragrance;
best in mild cli-
mates or with
protection in
Zone 6.
BELOW: 'Excelsa,'
1906 rambler, is
perfectly named.

Deciding which red climbing rose is the right one for you depends first on which red is pleasing to your eyes and in your setting. There are warm orange-reds and cool blue-reds, and there is also the length of the flowering season to consider. The almost breathtaking intensely pink-red 'Excelsa' appears only once in late spring or early summer, as does the old-fashioned 'Paul's Scarlet Climber.'

'Don Juan' makes a brash representative for modern, large-flowered, everblooming climbing roses. Developed by Malandrone of Italy and introduced in 1958, it is a luscious dark red—some say "black"—rose that is generously fragrant and appears on long stems for cutting.

'Climbing Playgirl' (not pictured) puts quite a different spin on "red," for it is an intense pink-magenta, a color once hated, now courted in gardens (for harmonizing with chartreuse). The flowers are big ruffly singles displaying eyecatching, scintillating golden center stamens.

'Red Fountain' is an excellent velvety red climber with strong fragrance and dark green foliage on canes that grow to 15 feet. For romance in a red-flowered climbing rose hardly any other can match 'Climbing Etoile de Hollande' with its bright crimson, Damask-scented flowers. The plant grows to 18 feet and blooms mostly in spring and fall.

ABOVE: 'Paul's Scarlet' is an old rambler rose, nearly thornless, that blooms once in early summer. Crossed with 'Gruss an Teplitz' in 1932, the result was 'Blaze,' which gardeners sometimes referred to as the everblooming 'Paul's Scarlet.' 'Blaze Improved,' more constant in bloom, has succeeded both.

NEXT PAGE: (LEFT) 'Parade' is a scented, modern climber from American breeder Eugene Boerner, 1953; (RIGHT) 'Lavender Lassie,' a 1960 hybrid musk from German breeder Kordes, has enough blue in its pink to suggest lavender. It grows readily and easily up to 8-12 ft. tall; it also tolerates more shade than most.

Critics Choice

Red is not the only rose color subject to different interpretations and expressions. There is the lemon yellow of 'Golden Showers,' the paler, butter yellow of 'Lady Banks Yellow,' and the veering-toward-apricot of 'Graham Thomas.' The buff-yellow-tinged-pink, fragrant flowers of 'Rêve d'Or' are another spin on the genre. Yellow roses can also turn up looking like white ones, and vice versa, much depending on time of day and season.

'Climbing Aloha' is the producer of voluptuous roses, rose-pink, tinged magenta, that smell delightful. Sometimes everblooming, and the producer of bronzy red foliage, it is no wonder 'Climbing Aloha' continues to be one of the most-loved modern climbing roses (1949).

'Pinata,' introduced in the United States in 1978 from Japanese breeder Suzuki, is also a modern, everblooming climber that produces exhibition-style double flowers on strong canes. What may be lacking in the "slight" fragrance is made up for in the sassy combination of yellow and vermilion that flatters most garden architecture.

One of the most elegant and refined climbing roses is 'Handel' whose exhibition-style flowers are white with bright red edging. They appear on old and new wood, have light fragrance, and grow on canes 12 to 15 feet long.

ABOVE: 'Pinata' is a modern climber, bred by Suzuki of Japan, introduced 1978. It is lightly fragrant, everblooming, and responsive to training.

Training

TRAIN A CLIMBING ROSE IN THE WAY IT SHOULD go and it will be a joy for the next year, but not forever. Nothing succeeds with a climbing rose like starting with a vision of what is to be, provided whatever structure is used will guide and support the desired result. Once yearly processing through the canes is introduced, the energy can be concentrated on the next flowering.

The vision achieved is better if the habit of the rose is suited to the shape it is to become. The stronger the growth, and the more vigorous the thrust upward, the better suited to large structures and gardens. A rose with the high beauty quotient of say 'Lady Banks Yellow' can, in the right climate and situation outgrow everything in sight.

The climbing forms of large-flowered hybrid roses such as 'Peace' are more suited to training on a wall, rather than twisted around a low fence railing or the swoop of a garland. They are better suited to fanning out.

Climbing roses, the same as bush roses, can be purchased bare root for spring planting or in containers for planting at any time the ground can be worked. The long canes expected of them begin to develop in the first season, but they do not hit their stride until the second year of growth and beyond.

AT LEFT: 'Excelsa' rambler roses play a leading role in the Rose Arc Garden at the Brooklyn Botanic Garden, in Brooklyn, New York.

AT LEFT: Training large-flowered climber 'Altissimo' stems into a horizontal fan shape promotes flowering of all laterals, almost continuously.

AT RIGHT, ABOVE AND BELOW: Horizontalization of climbing roses creates a multitude of short-stemmed, strong blooms that originate from the laterals. Instead of a vertical stem bearing one bouquet, there can be many.

AT RIGHT: Father Hugo's rose, *Rosa xanthina f. hugonis*, was brought to the West from China in 1899. Espaliering on a stone wall plays up year-round beauty: spring flowers, fernlike leaves, bronzy-orange fall foliage, bronzy-brown stems.

The roses illustrated opposite show the two basic situations where climbing roses are expected to grow, on a support in the open and against a wall or latticed structure.

No coincidence, 'Altissimo,' a fresh-air fiend that would languish tied to a wall, is shown growing freely along a fence beside an open road. By contrast, blooming gloriously against an old limestone wall is Father Hugo's rose. Also known as the 'Golden Rose of China,' it is well suited to stressful situations, and is even able to grow in impoverished soils, in part because the leaves, which are small and delicate appearing, and fernlike to the touch, are extremely tolerant of high temperatures and still air.

The two modern English roses on this page show the effect of horizontalizing the main canes so the laterals are activated. The result is evident in both photographs: Numerous secondary branches have formed show table-quality flowers on sturdy growths along the main cane.

Various materials are available for tying rose canes in place. Frugal gardeners have been known to make do with old nylon stockings. Rosarians favor natural jute or the same thing dyed green. Green plastic plant tie material has some give to it that permits growth without girdling.

The stronger the climbing rose, the stronger its support needs to be. Galvanized pipe, metal pieces welded together and painted, and concrete reinforcing rods are all used in building super structures to support exceptionally vigorous climbing roses. With any of these materials it is possible to paint or otherwise camouflage them so as not to detract, particularly in winter, when the canes are leafless. In fact, the effect can be subtly beautiful, even serenely hopeful, when the garden lies under a blanket of snow.

Rambler roses such as 'Excelsa' and 'Tausendschoen' send up new canes from the ground at the beginning of summer, following the once-yearly flowering in late spring. These growths are long and pliable, easily wound around posts, pillars, metal arches, and swoops of rope in festoons. The tricky part is this: The rosarian must patiently sort out, unravel, and remove the previously flowered canes; then guide, wrap, and tie-in the new canes. This must be done calmly and painstakingly—the stems are lax but not lacking thorns.

FAR LEFT: Climbing roses on an arbor lend special interest to the structure in winter. LEFT: Rambler roses in early midsummer are ready to be tied in. ABOVE: Flowered canes have been removed, new ones are tied in, and all is shipshape for another year.

ROSES ON THE ROCKS

WILD ROSES GROW *in the company of rocks, so, it is no surprise, the two display a natural affinity in gardens. If a rock outcropping is the background for a bed, a vigorous climber can be set at the front of its base, and the canes attached to disport the roses over and up the rocks' surface. This arrangement works for a wall that receives a half day or more of direct sunlight- best if this includes the cooler morning hours.*

If the wall faces north or is otherwise shaded, an alternative is to set the climbing roses on the dark side of the wall and train the canes toward the light. This can mean a big show along the crest and eventually draping the sunny facade or side of the wall. Some of the best choices for siting this way include 'Aloha,' 'Danse de Feu,' 'Dortmund,' 'Gloire de Dijon,' 'Golden Showers,' 'Kathleen Harrop,' 'Maigold,' 'Mermaid,' 'Madame Alfred Carrière,' 'Parade,' 'New Dawn,' and 'Zephirine Drouhin.'

ABOVE: Climbing roses trained up and over a rock wall, as seen from the side facing north. They will flower mainly on top and swoop down the other side to great effect, as backdrop for a topiary garden.

BELOW: 'Ivy Alice,' a 1927 sport of 'Excelsa,' has become a rare, collector's rose. Here it follows the lines of the archway on which the stems are annually trained. Together, they give the garden structure and beauty all year.

RESOURCES

Some North American Rosebush Suppliers & Specialists

Bridges Roses
2734 Toney Road
Lawndale, NC 28090
704.538.9412; catalog $1

W. Atlee Burpee & Co.
300 Park Ave.
Warminster, PA 18974-0001
800.333.5808; catalog free

Butner's Old Mill Nursery
806 South Belt Highway
St. Joseph, MO 64507
816.279.7434; catalog free

Carroll Gardens, Inc.
444 East Main Street
P.O. Box 310, Westminster, MD 21158
410.848.5422; catalog $3

Donovan's Roses
P.O. Box 37800
Shreveport, LA 71133-7800
318.861.6693; catalog for SASE

Hardy Roses of the North
Box 9
Danville, WA 99121-0009
250.442.8442

Hidden Springs Nursery
170 Hidden Springs Lane
Cookeville, TN 38501;
catalog $1

Historical Roses
1657 West Jackson Street
Painesville, OH 44077
216.357.7270 (SASE for catalog)

Hortico, Inc.
723 Robson Rd.
Waterdown, ON L0R 2H1
Canada 905.689.6984;
catalog $3

Interstate Nurseries
1706 Morrissey Drive
Bloomington, IL 61704

Jackson & Perkins Co.
1 Rose Lane
Medford, OR 97501
1.800.USA.ROSE

Kelly Nurseries
410 8th Ave. N.W.
Faribault, MN 55021
507.334.1623

Louisiana Nursery
Route 7, Box 43
Opelousas, LA 70570
318.948.3696; catalog $6

Lowe's Own-Root Roses
6 Sheffield Road
Nashua, NH 03062;
catalog $2

Mini-Rose Garden
P.O. Box 203
Cross Hill, SC 29332
864.998.4331

Moore Sequoia Nursery
2519 E. Noble
Visalia, CA 83282
209.732.0190; catalog free

Nor'East Miniature Roses, Inc.
P.O. Box 307
Rowley, MA 01969
508.948.7964

Northland Rosarium
9405 S. Williams Lane
Spokane, WA 99224
E-mail cparton@ior.com

Park Seed
Cokesbury Road
Greenwood, SC 29647-0001
864.223.7333

Pickering Nurseries, Inc.
670 Kingston Road
Pickering, Ont. L1V 1A6
Canada
905.839.2111; catalog $4

Plants of the Southwest
Aqua Fria, Route 6,
Box 11A
Santa Fe, NM 87501;
catalog $3.50

Rose Acres
6641 Crystal Boulevard
El Dorado, CA 95623-4804
916.626.1722

Roseraie at Bayfields, The
P.O. Box R
Waldoboro, ME 04572
207.832.6330;
narrated video catalog $9

Roses & Wine
3528 Montclair Road
Cameron Park, CA 95682
916.677.9722

Spring Hill Nurseries
110 W. Elm Street
Tipp City, OH 45371

Spring Valley Roses
N7637 330th Street
P.O. Box 7
Spring Valley, WI 54767
715.778.4481

Wayside Gardens
1 Garden Lane
Hodges, SC 29695-0001
800.845.1124

White Flower Farm
P.O. Box 50
Litchfield, CT 06759-0050
800.503.9624; catalog $4

Rose Society and Competitions

American Rose Society
P.O. Box 3900
Shreveport, LA 71130-0030
318.938.5402

All-America Rose Selections, Inc.
221 N. LaSalle St., Suite 3900
Chicago, IL 60601
312.372.7090

Metric Conversions
APPROXIMATE

TEMPERATURE				LENGTH		
WHEN YOU KNOW	MULTIPLY BY	TO FIND		WHEN YOU KNOW	MULTIPLY BY	TO FIND
$°F$ / Fahrenheit temp.	5/9 (-32)	Celsius temp. / $c°$		in. / inches	2.54	centimeters / CM
$°c$ / Celsius temp.	9/5 (+32)	Fahrenheit temp. / $F°$		ft. / feet	30	centimeters / CM